Princess
COLORING BOOK

ILLUSTRATIONS BY:

FAIRY CROCS

YOUNG Dreamers Press

DREAM. INSPIRE. CREATE.

VISIT US ONLINE:
www.youngdreamerspress.com

TAG US IN YOUR PHOTOS & VIDEOS:
www.instagram.com/youngdreamerspress
www.tiktok.com/@youngdreamerspress

WE'RE ALSO ON FACEBOOK:
www.facebook.com/youngdreamerspress

©2021 YOUNG DREAMERS PRESS
ALL RIGHTS RESERVED.

ISBN-13: 978-1-990136-03-0

NO PART OF THIS PUBLICATION MAY BE REPRODUCED, DISTRIBUTED, OR TRANSMITTED IN ANY FORM OR BY ANY MEANS INCLUDING PHOTOCOPYING, RECORDING, OR OTHER ELECTRONIC OR MECHANICAL METHODS, WITHOUT THE PRIOR WRITTEN PERMISSION OF THE PUBLISHER, EXCEPT IN THE CASE OF BRIEF QUOTATIONS EMBODIED IN CRITICAL REVIEWS AND CERTAIN OTHER NON-COMMERCIAL USES PERMITTED BY COPYRIGHT LAW.

BFF
HAPPY

BUT WAIT, THERE'S MORE!

VISIT GO.YOUNGDREAMERSPRESS.COM/PRINCESS

To join our newsletter and
make their world more colorful with
free printable coloring pages!

All pages sized for 8.5 x 11 paper and include a wide range of subjects including:
animals, kittens, mermaids, unicorns, mandalas, an astronaut, planets,
a firetruck, a construction vehicle, cupcakes, and more!

978-1-990136-07-8

978-1-990136-04-7

978-1-990136-05-4

978-1-990136-06-1

978-1-989790-36-6

978-1-989790-96-0

978-1-990136-02-3

978-1-989790-94-6

978-1-989790-69-4

978-1-990136-01-6

Also Available from

Young Dreamers Press

www.youngdreamerspress.com

978-1-989387-13-9

978-1-989387-46-7

978-1-989387-94-8

978-1-989387-96-2

978-1-989790-09-0

978-1-989790-13-7

978-1-989790-41-0

978-1-989790-64-9

978-1-989387-87-0

978-1-989387-88-7

978-1-777375-33-1

978-1-990136-03-0

978-1-989790-93-9

978-1-989790-95-3

978-1-777375-31-7

978-1-777375-32-4

Made in the USA
Las Vegas, NV
29 May 2021

23893689R20037